TABLE OF CONTENTS

USING THE BOOK:

Projects were selected to introduce a variety of aspects of American Indian Life. They are designed to use materials which are easily obtained. For reference and possible substitution, authentic materials are mentioned in the HISTORICAL AIDS.

Individuals, small or large groups, may successfully utilize this book.

ISBN 1-56472-000-4

American Indian Activity Book
© Edupress • 33181 Santiago Drive • Dana Point, CA 92629

WOVEN MAT

HISTORICAL AID:

Weaving was a skill shared by many Indian tribes. Mats woven without looms
were made by the Prairie, Lakes, and Northeastern tribes. Mats, made from bark,
husks, twigs, and other natural materials were used as roofs, partitions, and
floor coverings.   They could also serve as clothing, sails, and tool wrappers.

MATERIALS:

2 shades brown construction paper, each 9" x 12"
Glue
Twigs, bark, leaves

DIRECTIONS:

Cut one piece of paper into strips 1/2" x 9".

Fold second sheet in half.

Beginning at fold, cut to about one inch from open end;

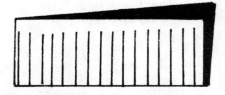

Lay paper flat.

Using 1/2" strip, weave
through flat paper, over-
under, over-under, until
opposite edge is reached.

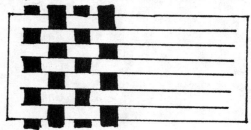

Repeat procedure.

When complete, tuck twigs, bark, and leaves into weaving.

Glue into place.

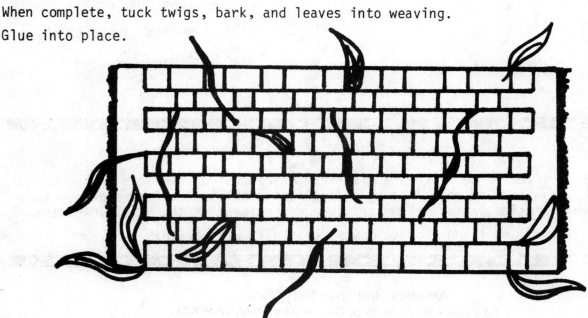

PICTURE WRITING

HISTORICAL AID:

To the Indian, a symbol was more than a design, it was a way of communicating and expressing beliefs. Symbolic designs were applied to their horses, bodies, homes, arts and crafts. They were placed on weapons with the belief that should the weapon itself not protect them from harm, the symbol would. Symbols enabled individuals to communicate, and a tribe to write their history. Symbols varied from tribe to tribe. Those shown here are suggestions for use with various projects throughout the book.

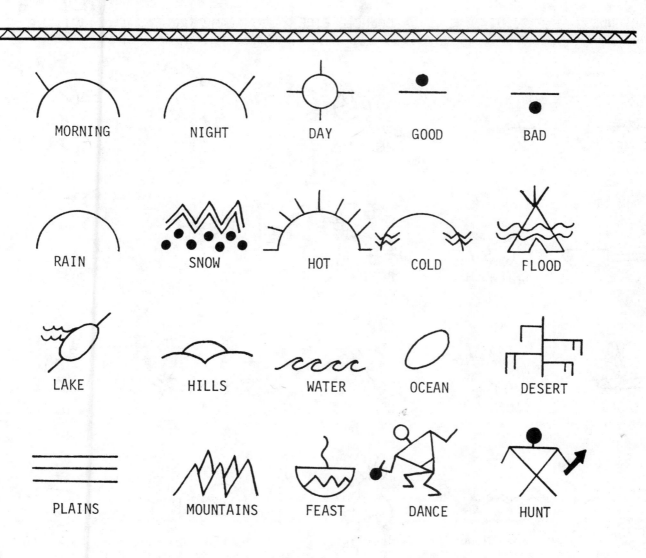

MORNING	NIGHT	DAY	GOOD	BAD
RAIN	SNOW	HOT	COLD	FLOOD
LAKE	HILLS	WATER	OCEAN	DESERT
PLAINS	MOUNTAINS	FEAST	DANCE	HUNT

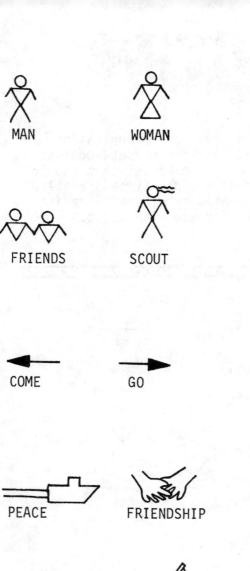

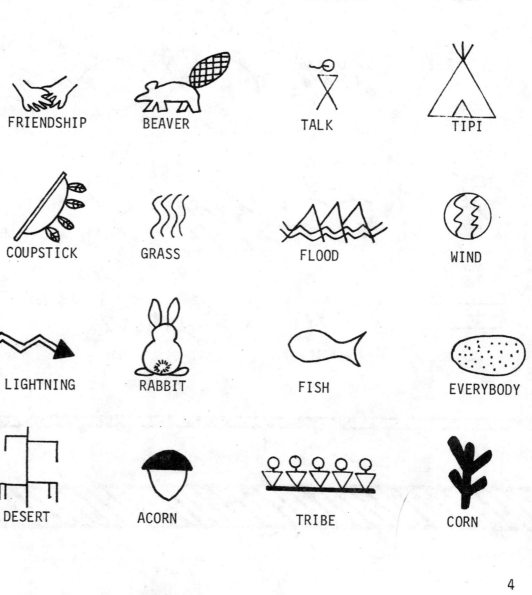

MAN WOMAN BROTHERS SISTERS STRENGTH

FRIENDS SCOUT COUNCIL FIRE CAMPFIRE VILLAGE

COME GO MEDICINE SICKNESS WAR

PEACE FRIENDSHIP BEAVER TALK TIPI

LEADER COUPSTICK GRASS FLOOD WIND

CLOUD LIGHTNING RABBIT FISH EVERYBODY

BLANKET DESERT ACORN TRIBE CORN

THUNDERBIRD

HISTORICAL AID:

In Indian mythology, the Thunderbird was believed to be a powerful spirit responsible for the water that nurtured the earth and made things grow. The Indians believed that lightning came from its mouth and thunder was made from the beating of its wings. It was also believed that the Thunderbird carried water on its back which brought rain. Because it was believed to be so important, the Thunderbird symbol appeared frequently in all phases of Indian life.

MATERIALS:

Construction paper
9" x 12" black
2" x 2" yellow
9" x 6" red
1" x 2" orange
Scissors
Glue

DIRECTIONS:

Fold red paper in half. Starting at the fold, cut as shown by the dotted lines. Open and glue, centered, to black.

Use red scraps to cut 3 triangles, approximately 1" at base and 2" tall. Glue triangles following color code.

Round edges of yellow square to make a circle. Glue.

Cut orange diagonally to form 2 triangles. Glue as shown.

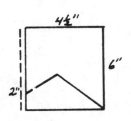

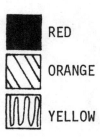

WINTER COUNT

HISTORICAL AID:

The Plains Indians used the Winter Count or calendar as a record of tribal events. Since the tribes counted years by winters, the name Winter Count was given. Hides were suspended between poles or tree trunks and symbols were written on the hides depicting important events each year. This record told the tribes' history. Winter Counts were then passed on from generation to generation.

MATERIALS:

Brown paper lunch bag (to simulate animal hide)
Paint brush   Water   Crayons

DIRECTIONS:

Open bag along seam, cut off bottom and lay flat.

Dip paint brush in water and paint a water line about 1" from outer edge of sack. (Each child's line will be different.)

Tear along wet outline to form ragged edges.

Roll sack into ball to wrinkle, then open and lay flat.

Choose five or six symbols to display on your sack (animal hide). Some symbols are shown. Children can create their own.

Using crayon, heavily draw the various designs on the sack.

6

CALENDAR STICK

HISTORICAL AID:

One method used by Indians for keeping a record of the passing of time was with a calendar stick. A notch was made on the flat side for each month (moon). Notches made in the sides represented years. At the sound of the first thunder of the season, the first yearly notch was cut. Often there was a side on the stick for each family member.

MATERIALS:

Popsicle sticks   Marking pen

DIRECTIONS:

Using the symbols below, mark the stick to show the passing of time.

As more sticks are needed, glue them together at the ends.

1 day (sun)

1 month (moon)

1 year (winter or Great Sun)

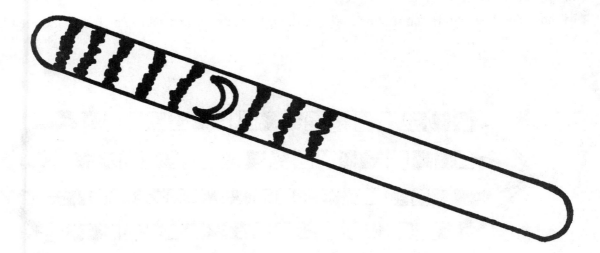

WAMPUM BELT

HISTORICAL AID:

Wampum was the name used mainly by the Eastern Indians for white, purple, or black beads made from shells. Wampum was woven into belts and clothing and was originally worn as decoration, symbolizing wealth and power. The color of the bead had meaning: white stood for health, peace, and riches, purple and black for sympathy or sorrow. With the coming of the white man, Wampum served as money for trading. The dark beads were often considered more valuable. Belts of Wampum were also exchanged during the signing of a treaty or agreement as a sign of good faith.

MATERIALS:

Salad macaroni   Black and purple ink   Yarn or string
                                                       (about 10')

DIRECTIONS:

Divide macaroni into thirds.

Soak one-third in black ink, one-third in purple ink, leaving remaining macaroni plain. Allow to dry.

Cut 4 pieces of string large enough to fit around the waist, plus 8".

String macaroni, alternating colors, leaving 4" of string at each end.

Tie a knot in string at each end, as close to the macaroni as possible, large enough to hold macaroni in place.

Tie the four strands together, about an inch from the macaroni at each end.

SEED NECKLACE

Indian jewelry was made by stringing natural substances together. Such items used for neck or wrist adornment were nuts, berries, porcupine quills, dried animal bones, seashells, stones and seeds. Eventually, the white man introduced porcelain and glass beads which were intricately woven into designs.

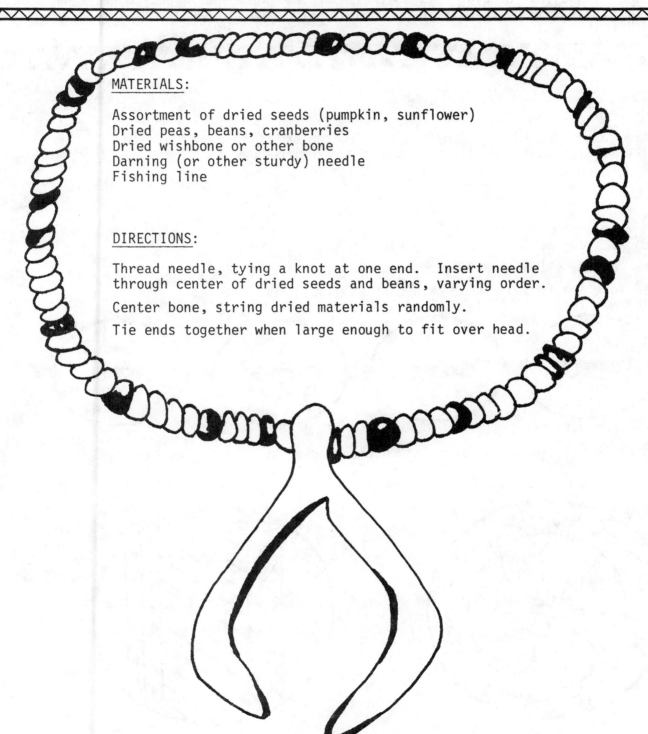

MATERIALS:

Assortment of dried seeds (pumpkin, sunflower)
Dried peas, beans, cranberries
Dried wishbone or other bone
Darning (or other sturdy) needle
Fishing line

DIRECTIONS:

Thread needle, tying a knot at one end. Insert needle through center of dried seeds and beans, varying order.

Center bone, string dried materials randomly.

Tie ends together when large enough to fit over head.

CONCHO BELT

HISTORICAL AID:

Concho discs were originally worn by the Eastern Indians as ornaments. War and trade brought the discs to the Navaho. The Navaho, as reknowned silversmiths, continued to make conchos of silver in circular and oval shapes engraving them both simply and intricately. Six to twelve conchos were then laced together with leather thongs into belts which were worn by both men and women.

MATERIALS:

Lightweight cardboard   Tin foil   Toothpick
Shoelace (leather or cloth) to fit waist.   Holepuncher

DIRECTIONS:

Cut 8 discs out of cardboard, same size as shown at bottom.

Punch 2 holes, slightly off-center.

Thread shoelace in and out of each disc until all are attached, spacing evenly.

Cover discs with tin foil.

Using toothpick, "engrave" a design onto each disc by pressing gently.

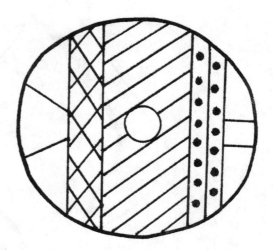

NAVAHO   PLAINS

SHAMAN MASK

HISTORICAL AID:

The Shaman was an important figure in the tribe. He conducted religious ceremonies but was respected mainly for the magical powers he was believed to have. Among these powers was supposedly the power of healing the sick thus the Shaman also earned the name "Medicine Man". Iroquois Shamans belonged to a False Face Society and wore masks during ceremonies to chase away the demons that caused sickness. These masks were carved on the trunk of a living tree, usually basswood, and removed upon completion with the idea that a living spirit would enter the mask. These masks were designed to entertain rather than frighten.

MATERIALS:

Brown shopping bag
Assorted paints and brushes
Cornhusks, yarn, dried grass
Scissors
Glue
Stapler

DIRECTIONS:

Cut bag into any shape, large enough to cover face.

Paint exaggerated facial features onto bag.

Use cornhusks, yarn, or dried grass glued on as hair.

CEREMONIAL BANDS

HISTORICAL AID:

Arm, wrist, ankle, and head bands were worn by the Indians during ceremonials, dances, Pow-wows, and feasts. They were made from animal skins and adorned with painted designs, beads, shells, and feathers. The designs varied depending upon the use of the band either as proof of bravery, as sign of honor, or simply as an ornament of decoration. Eventually the white man brought bells and glass beads which were added to the various bands as decoration.

HEADBAND

MATERIALS:

2" strip of poster board or construction paper to fit head
Tempera paint, assorted colors
Feathers (real or made from construction paper)
2 - 3" x 3" construction paper, any color
Scissors
Glue
Stapler

DIRECTIONS:

Paint a design on the band.

Staple to fit head.

Cut 2 circles from construction paper. Glue to opposite sides of band.

Glue feathers to circles. If making feathers from construction paper, cut from 2" x 6" paper, fringe.

ARMBAND

MATERIALS:

Colored paper strip 1" x 10" for band
5 colored squares, 5", 4", 3", 2", and 1"
Feathers
Glue   Crayons   Scissors

DIRECTIONS:

Decorate a paper strip with Indian symbols using crayons.

Cut colored squares of various sizes into circles and fringe the edges.

Decorate the smallest circle with a special geometric design.

Arrange circles from the largest to the smallest and glue on strip.

Decorate with feathers coming out of the discs.

Fit armband and staple.

ANKLEBAND

MATERIALS:

Yarn
Scissors

DIRECTIONS:

Cut 60 - 7" strips yarn.

Cut 1 - 12" strip.

Loop strips as illustrated over 12" piece of yarn.

Place loops close together.

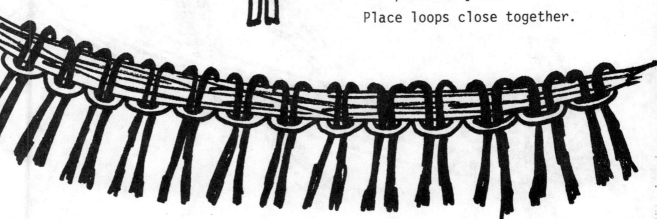

HISTORICAL AID:

Also called a "War Hatchet", the tomahawk had several uses. It served not only as
a weapon but also as a tool and an expression of peace during ceremonials.
Brightly decorated, some tomahawks were buried during peacetime and dug up during
war, thus the expression ending an argument, "Bury the Hatchet". As with many
American Indian crafts, the style of tomahawk varied from tribe to tribe. Following
are two distinctly different types.

SPIKED-CLUB

Carved from wood, the Spiked-club tomahawk was used widely in ceremonials by the
Iroquois. It was basically flat with a 4" deer horn spike attached. It was
brightly decorated with painted designs and feathers.

MATERIALS:

Cardboard 4" x 24"   Paints, assorted colors
Feathers, real or made from construction paper
Paint Brush   Scissors   Glue

DIRECTIONS:

Cut cardboard as shown at right, making 4" spike
from scraps.

Paint both sides of cardboard with Indian symbols
and designs.

Glue feathers and spike to ends and sides of
cardboard.

PIPE TOMAHAWK

The Pipe Tomahawk was used both as a weapon and for smoking tobacco. It became known as the "Peacepipe" as it was passed from man to man in many tribes when an agreement or treaty was signed. It was also a deadly weapon that was handed down through generations with the bloody stories behind it being retold over and over again. The original pipe was made by lashing a sharpened head of flint or bronze to a hollowed-out stick. The white man brought to the Indian, iron which replaced the original heads making the tomahawk much sharper and stronger.

MATERIALS:

Newspaper	Cardboard 4" x 8"	Twine
Tempera paint, black and brown		
Glue	Masking tape	Scissors

DIRECTIONS:

Roll a folded sheet of newspaper to form a hollow tube about 18" long.

Secure with masking tape.

Paint tube brown. Allow to dry.

Cut 2 cardboard hatchet heads and paint black.

Glue ends of heads together, one on each side of tube, extending past tube. Do not glue together at top.

Use twine to lash head to handle.

COUP STICK

HISTORICAL AID:

The coup stick was an honor stick used for "counting coup" (pronounced 'coo') in battle. A coup was earned by the warrior who was able to touch an enemy in battle with hand or stick and not kill him. For this the warrior earned a Coup Feather, often the beautiful feather from the revered eagle. There were many types of coup sticks depending on tribes and regions. The one shown below was also used as a battle flag. It was made by attaching a leather or animal skin thong to the ends of a stick. Feathers were then attached in a "clothesline" fashion to the thong.

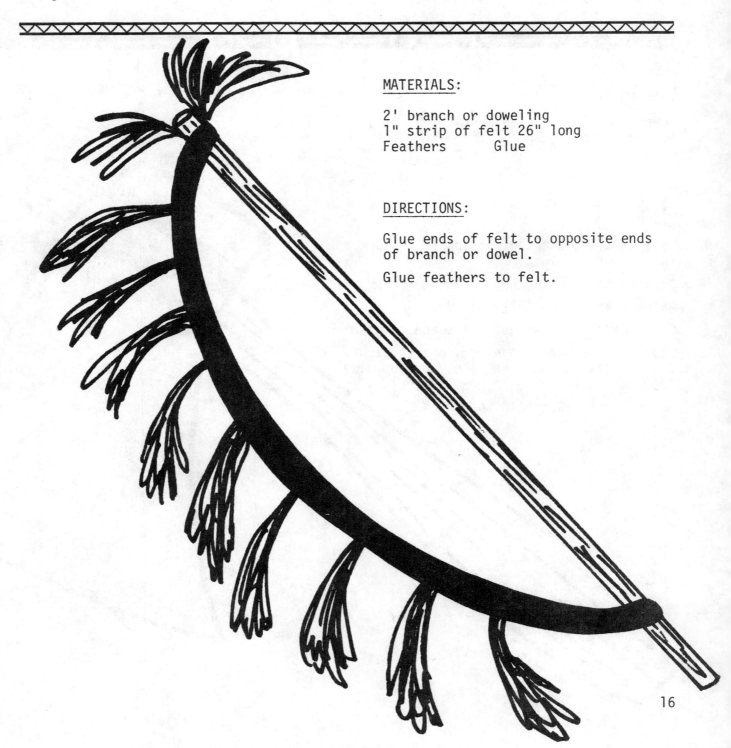

MATERIALS:

2' branch or doweling
1" strip of felt 26" long
Feathers   Glue

DIRECTIONS:

Glue ends of felt to opposite ends of branch or dowel.

Glue feathers to felt.

ARROWHEAD

HISTORICAL AID:

The tip attached to the end of the an arrow shaft was called an arrowhead. The addition of this tip created both a weapon and a hunting instrument. Arrowheads were made from many types of hard stones such as flint, obsidian, slate, and quartz. Small pieces were hammered off a larger stone then chipped with an antler or bone until the desired shape and degree of sharpness was reached. The length of the arrowhead varied from 1/2" to 2". Stone arrowheads were later replaced by iron with the advent of trade with the white man.

MATERIALS:

Bar of soap
Plastic knife

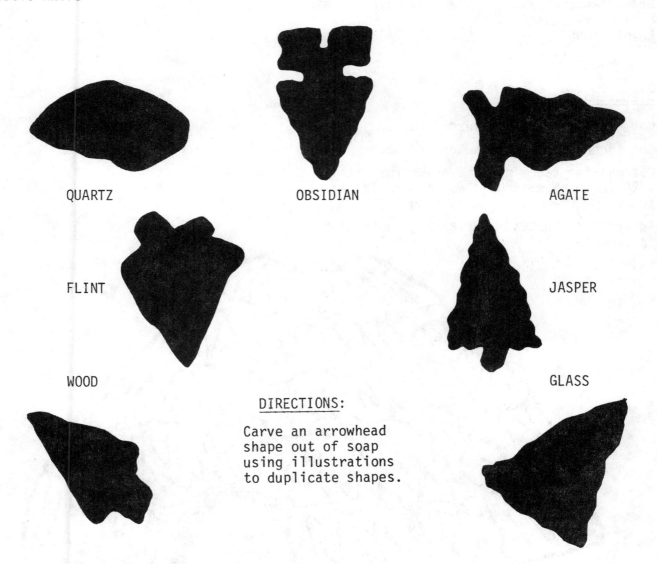

QUARTZ   OBSIDIAN   AGATE

FLINT   JASPER

WOOD   GLASS

DIRECTIONS:

Carve an arrowhead
shape out of soap
using illustrations
to duplicate shapes.

WICKIUP

HISTORICAL AID:

The wickiup of the desert-dwelling Plains Indians was very similar to the wigwam of the Eastern and Great Lakes Indians. They were both cone-shaped or domed structures built on a framework of saplings and covered with brush, bark, dirt, or skins. Size ranged from 8 - 15' in diameter and 7' high at the center. The doorway was not covered and there was a hole in the center of the roof so that smoke from the family fireplace could escape easily.

MATERIALS:

Margarine or Cool Whip tub, preferably large
Brown tempera paint diluted to "wash" consistency
Masking tape, any width
Paint brush

DIRECTIONS:

Cut door opening in inverted tub.

Cut circular opening in top of tub.

Cut masking tape into pieces approximately 1/2" long. Number will depend on size of tub.

Adhere tape to tub, overlapping, until tub is covered.

Paint tape.

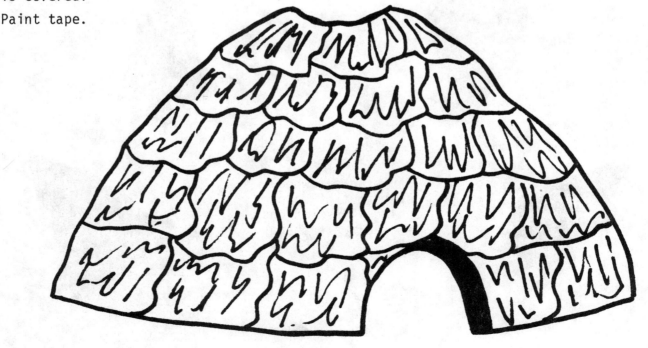

HOGAN

HISTORICAL AID:

The Navahos dwelt in "hogans", six-sided structures built from horizontally laid logs, sometimes covered with packed earth. There were only two openings, one in the domed roof as a way of letting smoke from the central fireplace to escape, and one as a doorway. Doors always faced east, to the rising sun, according to Navaho myth. In winter, doorways would be covered with blankets to keep out the cold.

MATERIALS:

9" x 9" brown construction or butcher paper or paper bag
Approximately 60 sticks (popsicle, small twigs)
Glue   Scissors   Dried weeds (optional)

DIRECTIONS:

Break 3 sticks into pieces about 1/2" long.

Arrange 6 sticks into hexagonal shape, leaving opening, and diameter of about 8".

Glue small pieces to bottom edge of one stick nearest opening.

Begin gluing by alternating sticks top and and bottom. The stick with the smaller piece attached will be the first top piece, then work in a circular manner. Stick will extend where they join. Continue until sides are 7 sticks high. Small pieces will need to be used only at door openings where there is no other stick to give height.

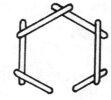

Cut square as shown. Make slit on dotted line making a center circle about 2 1/2" in diameter.

Overlap edges to make round dome leaving circle open in top.

Attach roof to "log" base, by gluing.

Optional: Glue dried weeds to roof to give covered brush effect.

 Tipi

HISTORICAL AID:

The "tipi" was a portable home used by nomadic tribes of the Plains such as the Commanche and Sioux. Tipis were cone shaped, built around a structure of poles placed in a tripod fashion then covered with animal skins. Tipis were ordinarily 10' x 12' high and some were painted with symbols depicting great tribal events. The fireplace was in the center with a hole in the top of the tipi for smoke to escape.

MATERIALS:

Large margarine tub lid (6" diameter)
7" x 16" rectangle paper bag or tan butcher paper
Water
Scotch tape
6 popsicle sticks
6" string or thin yarn
Scissors

DIRECTIONS:

Place lid with lip up. Taping the lid to desk to secure will help with the next step.

Place sticks vertically against lip at 3" intervals. Tape temporarily to hold. Lean sticks to center until they meet. Use string to lash sticks together leaving about 1/2" of stick extending.

Draw crayon designs on bag.

Wet bag completely and crumple. Open.

While bag is still wet, mold around stick "framework", leaving space between 2 of the sticks as a doorway. Wrap paper under the lid.

LONGHOUSE

The "longhouse" was the dwelling of the Northeastern Iroquois Indians. It was a rectangular structure built on a pole framework and covered with cedar planking or overlapped bark. The roofs were either domed or peaked. The longhouse was usually around 60' long x 18' high. It had one hallway down its center with rooms off each side where individual families lived. Supplies were kept in storage areas at the ends of the buildings. Families shared fireplaces.

MATERIALS:

1 - 12" x 14" brown construction paper
1 - 7" x 12" brown construction paper
2 - 6" x 7" brown construction paper
8 - 2" x 12" strips brown crepe paper
Scissors
Glue

DIRECTIONS:

Fold edges of 7" x 12" paper up (about 1/2") to make base.

Put glue on outside edges of upward fold.

Bend 12" x 14" paper and glue to base.

Cut 6" x 7" paper as shown at left by dotted lines.

Cut door openings.

Clip curved edges about 1/2", fold back, and glue to inside of house - clipping more as needed.

Cover curved top with crepe paper over-lapping to simulate bark.

CHICKEE

HISTORICAL AID:

The Chickee was a dwelling built by the Southeastern tribes such as the Seminole of Florida. These Indians depended on river life and thus their homes were often constructed on swampy lands. As a protection against rising rivers, the Chickee was built on poles with the floor platform above ground level. The roof was of palm fronds and the home had no sides. Cooking was done in a separate building hut shared by several families.

MATERIALS:

1 - 8" x 12" brown construction paper
1 - 6" x 8" brown construction paper or tag
48 - 1" x 2" green construction paper
8 paper drinking straws large opening
Glue
Scotch tape
Scissors
Holepunch

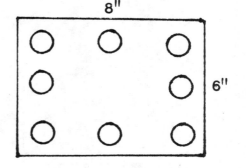

DIRECTIONS:

Punch holes in 6" x 8" paper as shown.

Cut 6 straws 5 1/2". Make a mark 1 1/2" from one end.

Insert 5 1/2" straws through side holes of tag or paper to 1 1/2" mark. Secure underneath with scotch tape.

Fold remaining rectangle in half.

Pinch straw opening at top.

Glue folded paper to straws, to form roof.

Make slashes in each of the small rectangles to simulate palm fronds. Beginning at lower edge of roof and working to top of roof, paste the rectangles, eight in a row, three rows, overlapping each row.

PUEBLO

HISTORICAL AID:

The Pueblo was an apartment-like dwelling built by the Pueblo Indians of the Southwest. It was constructed with adobe bricks. The size and number of stories varied but most Pueblos had at least one "kiva", an underground ceremonial room and meeting place. The pueblos were divided into rooms with the entrance on the rooftop. Originally fires were built in the center of a room with the smoke escaping through the entrance in the roof. Eventually the fireplace was moved to a corner and chimneys were constructed.

MATERIALS:

3 boxes without lids, graduated in size
Brown tempera paint
Red tempera paint
4 popsicle sticks
8 toothpicks
Masking tape
Glue
Paint brush
Scissors

DIRECTIONS:

Cut door opening in each box.

Mix brown and red paint to achieve brickmud color.

Paint outside of each box.

When paint dries, stack boxes and secure with masking tape. Paint tape.

Make ladders by placing popsicle sticks side-by-side and gluing toothpicks across at intervals for steps. Place ladders on "Pueblo".

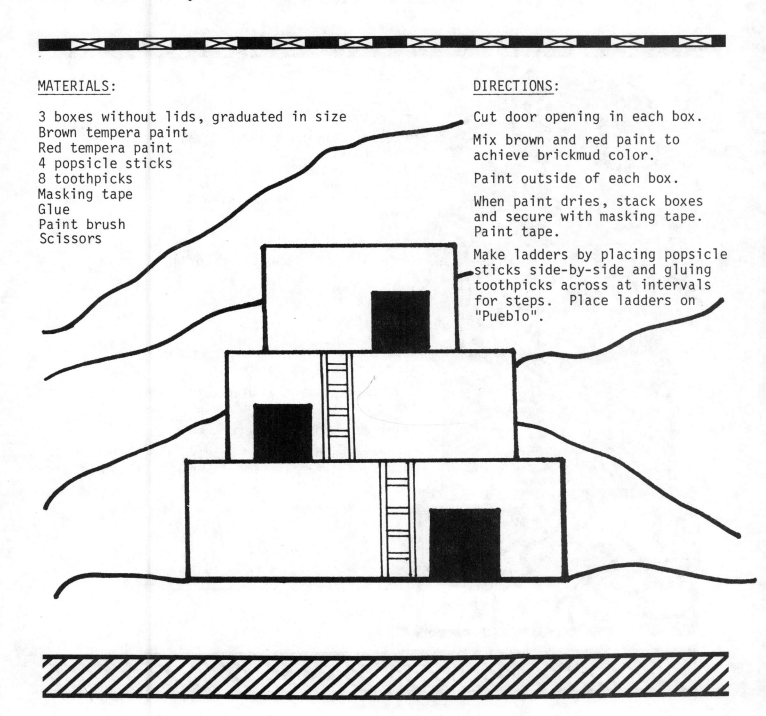

TOTEM POLE

HISTORICAL AID:

Totem poles, carved from timber and then painted, were erected by families within their village. Each pole had a different story to tell through the carving of animals or masks. Some were memorials to a head of a household while others related family history or tribal legends. Each clan was associated with a certain animal which appeared on the totem outside a home, making dwellings easily identifiable. Some poles, standing as tall as 50' were hollowed out to make handling easier. Originally, stone implements were used for carving to be replaced later by iron tools.

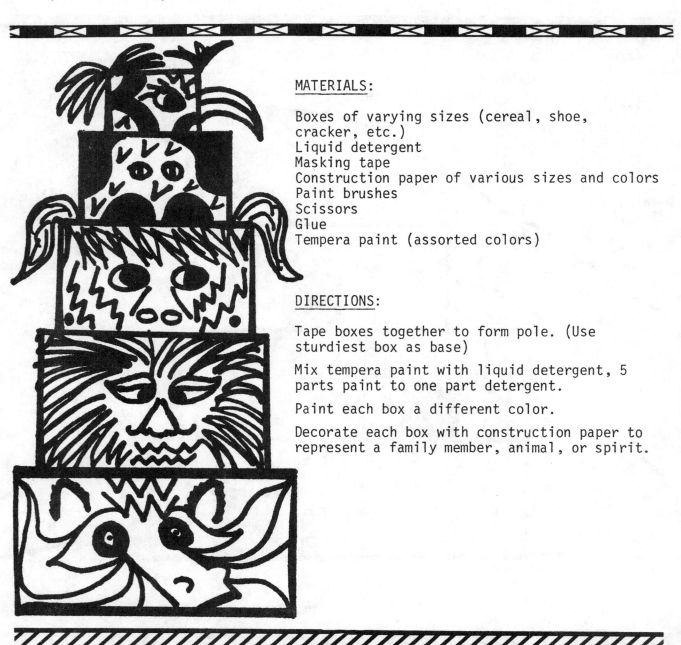

MATERIALS:

Boxes of varying sizes (cereal, shoe, cracker, etc.)
Liquid detergent
Masking tape
Construction paper of various sizes and colors
Paint brushes
Scissors
Glue
Tempera paint (assorted colors)

DIRECTIONS:

Tape boxes together to form pole. (Use sturdiest box as base)

Mix tempera paint with liquid detergent, 5 parts paint to one part detergent.

Paint each box a different color.

Decorate each box with construction paper to represent a family member, animal, or spirit.

COOKING BASKET

HISTORICAL AID:

Cooking equipment, made from available materials, ranged from very primitive to extremely imaginative. In California, a hole was dug in the ground and an animal skin was placed in the hole. Hot stones and water were added to boil foods. Southwestern tribes used water-tight baskets and pottery over a fire for boiling foods. The northern Forest people used a disposable cooking vessel (shown below) when they were on hunting expeditions. This type of basket was made by folding birch bark into a rectangular shape, lacing with a leather thong and adding a leather handle for hanging over a fire. After one use, the "pan" was thrown away.

MATERIALS:

Brown wrapping paper 18" x 36"
18" string   stapler

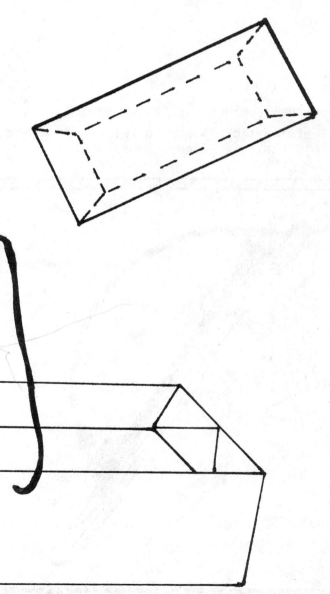

DIRECTIONS:

Make a 6" fold on all sides. Open.

Make an inward diagonal fold at each corner, until the sides form a right angle.

Staple in place at each end.

Tie a knot at each end of the string. Staple in place on opposite sides of basket.

UTENSILS

Eating utensils were not used extensively among the Indians. The majority simply used their hands. However, some utensils were inventively made from bone, shell or wood. Knives were sometimes chiseled from flint for skinning and cutting.

MATERIALS:

2 sticks or twigs
(Popsicle, tongue depressor)
1 Shell (clam, mussel)
String

DIRECTIONS:

Place shell between sticks or twigs.

Coil string tightly around twigs to hold shell in place. Knot.

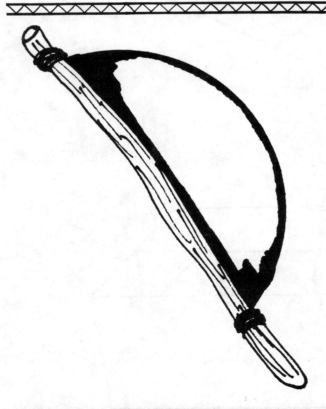

MATERIALS:

Tin foil
Cardboard cut in a half circle with tabs, as shown
String
Stick or twig

DIRECTIONS:

Cover cardboard with foil.

Attach to stick by coiling string around each tab. Knot securely.

RECIPES

HISTORICAL AID:

Cooking was simple. Roots, berries, and nuts made up a large part of the Indian diet which, of course, depended upon the tribe's region. Fruits, and meat from hunting were often dried in the sun to preserve for the cold winters of the East or the transient life of the Plains. Maple syrup was used frequently as a seasoning. Many plants and leaves were discovered to be edible. Cooking by roasting or boiling was done in watertight baskets or clay pots. Baking was done in adobe ovens or on flat stones laid over a fire.

WILD RICE CASSEROLE

Among the tribes of the Great Lakes Region, the most important food was wild rice, the seed of a shallow water grass, harvested just before the grain was ripe. After gathering the rice, it was dried in the sun and the kernels were danced upon to loosen the hull.

24 small servings

1 14 oz. package wild rice
1 cup blueberries
3 tbsp. maple syrup

Prepare rice according to package directions. Stir in blueberries and syrup.

PUDDING

30 small servings

5 - 16 oz. cans pumpkin or the pulp from a pumpkin, mashed and steamed.
5 apples, cored and cut in chunks
5 tbsp. maple syrup

Steam apples until soft. Mix with pumpkin. Add maple syrup. Heat in saucepan or warm in oven.

CORN MUSH

30 small servings

7 cups corn meal
2 red chili peppers dried and crushed
Water
Cornhusks

Mix corn meal, and chili peppers with enough water to make a consistency of paste. Wrap about 1/4 cup in each cornhusk. Heat until warm.

HISTORICAL AID:

Corn was a main food source in North American Indian cookery. Its uses varied from being eaten straight off the cob to boiling it to make a kind of corn coffee. (A bean mixture made by boiling beans with a lump of fat and adding green corn became a favorite dish of the English settlers.) Corn meal was made by pounding the kernels until they were a fine flour. The meal was made into corn cakes and cooked on a flat stone or wrapped in a corn husk and baked in ashes. Hominy, a basic Indian staple, was made by boiling corn with wood ashes, which loosened the hulls.

HOMINY

Soak 1 quart of shelled dried corn for 12 hours in 2 tbsp. baking soda. Bring the mixture to a boil and simmer for 3 hours or until the hulls loosen. Drain and rub corn until the hulls are taken off. Repeat the process.

HOMINY CAKES

2 cups hominy
2 tbsp. flour
1 egg

Mix ingredients and form into flat cakes. Fry in fat until browned.

JOURNEY CAKE (A flat cornbread taken travelling by Northeastern Indians.)

1 cup corn meal
1 tsp. salt
1 1/2 tsp. sugar
2 tbsp. fat (butter)
1 cup boiling water
1 egg

Add water to dry ingredients and mix. Add egg and beat. Make into small cakes and bake at 400° for 20 minutes.

POTLATCH

HISTORICAL AID:

A Potlatch was a Northwest Indian celebration held in honor of many things, the passing of a great chief, the birth of a son, the raising of a totem pole, the merging of two villages. Its name was derived from a Chinook word meaning "giving". The host chief traditionally gave elaborate gifts and presided over rituals. Hundreds of guests were invited with social rank determining the seating of family members. A special Potlatch building was erected within the village for these special occasions. The clothing worn was elaborate, the food abundant. Enjoy some of the foods that might have been offered at a Potlatch.

Popcorn	Pumpkin	Raspberries
Sunflower Seeds	Squash	Strawberries
Chestnuts	Lima Beans	Blackberries
Acorns	Kidney Beans	Blueberries
Hazelnuts	Corn	Maple Sugar Candy
Hickory Nuts	Mushrooms	Melons
Pinon Nut	Potatoes	
Turkey	Tomatoes	Hot Cocoa
Smoked Fish	Sweet Potatoes	Herbal Teas
Venison		
Rabbit		

SUCCOTASH ✽

Cook a mixture of lima or kidney beans and corn with a lump of fat.

STEW ✽

Boil fowl or fish, onions, carrots, potatoes, and squash together until cooked.

HERBS

HISTORICAL AID:

Sickness was believed to be caused by evil spirits or by the wicked use of
supernatural power. Medicine men tried to use charms, magic rituals, ceremonies,
and herbs in curing illness. Plants were dried then boiled to make a medicinal
liquid or tea. Roots, bark, and leaves were all included in Indian remedies.
Flowers were used mainly for ceremonials rather than medicinal purposes.

Experiment with the making of these herbal remedies. Their medicinal use is
listed, although usage is not suggested.

Crush the dried seeds or roots with a stone into pulp or a fine powder. Mix with
a little water to make a paste.

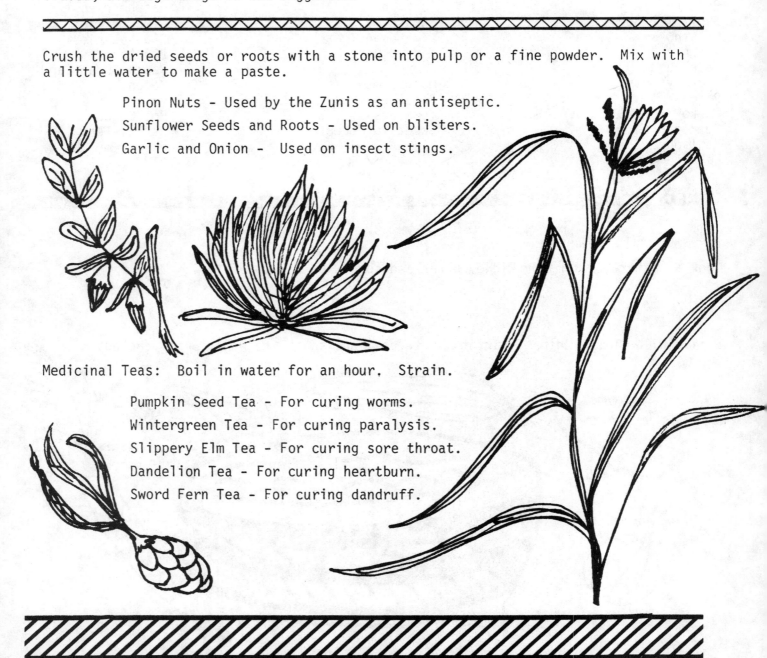

     Pinon Nuts - Used by the Zunis as an antiseptic.

     Sunflower Seeds and Roots - Used on blisters.

     Garlic and Onion - Used on insect stings.

Medicinal Teas: Boil in water for an hour. Strain.

     Pumpkin Seed Tea - For curing worms.

     Wintergreen Tea - For curing paralysis.

     Slippery Elm Tea - For curing sore throat.

     Dandelion Tea - For curing heartburn.

     Sword Fern Tea - For curing dandruff.

POTTERY

HISTORICAL AID:

The Indians of the Southwest began making pottery of clay or mud hundreds of years ago. The pottery of the Pueblo women has prevailed as the most famous. Originally, baskets were used as molds but eventually the coil method, used in this project, was developed. The shapes of the bowls varied, depending on the maker. Coiled bowls were smoothed inside and out, dried in the sun, and often painted with bright designs. The pottery was watertight and fireproof lending itself to many uses including eating and drinking vessels, cooking, storage, and carrying.

MATERIALS:

Self-hardening, air-drying modeling clay (found in craft stores)
Waxed paper
Enamel paints, assorted colors (optional)

DIRECTIONS:

Tear off a piece of waxed paper to place on work surface.

Put a small piece of clay on the waxed paper.

Begin rolling the clay with the flat palm of the hand until a long rope is made. It should be thick enough so as not to break when coiled.

Dip fingers in the water in order to keep the clay moist.

To form the base of the bowl, simply wrap the coils. Coils can be connected by wetting the ends and pressing them together.

When the desired base size has been made, begin working the coils upward. The simplest bowl is made with straight vertical sides.

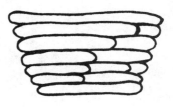

Wet fingers and smooth over coils inside and out.

Allow to dry for several days.

Paint with bright designs, if desired.

STAMP PRINTING

HISTORICAL AID:

Northeastern Indians decorated their baskets by stamp printing the designs
with natural objects. Twigs, seeds, shells, animal claws and bones, feathers,
and leather were rolled or bound together and then dipped in dye before
printing.

MATERIALS:

Assorted objects as named above
Paint, varied colors
Construction paper for printing

DIRECTIONS:

Dip edges of selected objects and press onto paper.

Remove carefully.

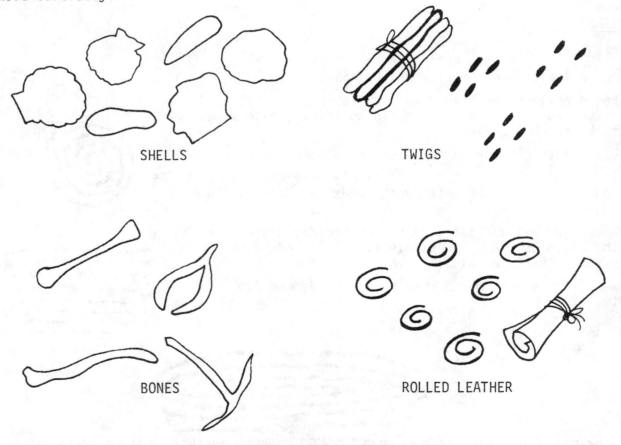

SHELLS

TWIGS

BONES

ROLLED LEATHER

RATTLE

HISTORICAL AID:

Musical instruments were an important part of Indian ceremonials. Drums and chanting provided a rhythmical background for the dancing and rituals that took place within each tribe. Rattles made from natural objects completed the musical sound. Rattles were commonly made filling gourds with dried beans, shells strung together, and bones attached to sticks.

MATERIALS:

12" stick or twig
String
8 objects - shells, bones, rocks, nut shells

DIRECTIONS:

Tie a piece of string to each object at 1" intervals. Tie objects onto stick.

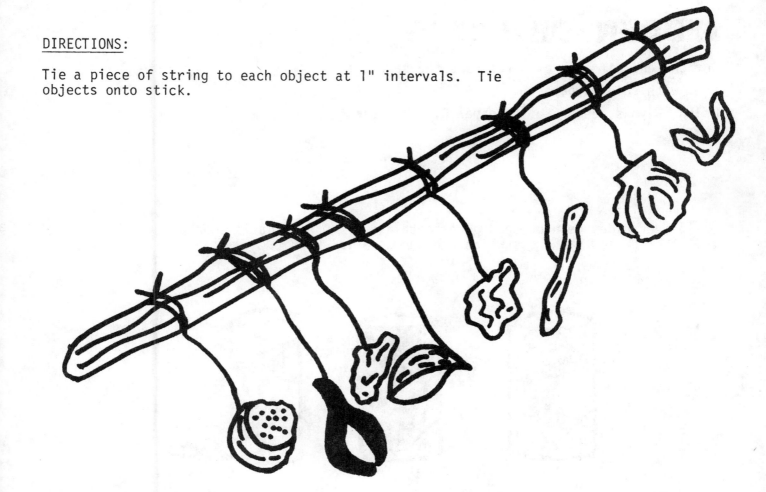

GAMES

HISTORICAL AID:

Once again the Indians utilized the natural objects around them in the creation
of their many games. Bones, twigs, and rocks cleverly became a child's plaything.
Races were often run using sticks and rocks passed from one runner to the next.
Some games were for individuals and small groups and some for hundreds of players.
Competition was fierce. Village would challenge village to a game of "Bagataway",
similar to present day Lacrosse. Many villages had great areas cleared to use
as a playing field. A ball was made by stuffing buckskin with buffalo hair.
Whatever the game, we can recognize many of their forms in our present day games.

HIDDEN OBJECT

Cut one end off each of three cans the same size.

Wrap with colored paper.

Using crayons, decorate the paper with symbols.

TO PLAY THE GAME:

One player hides bean or seed underneath a can. One point is scored if
the other person can guess which can the bean is under.

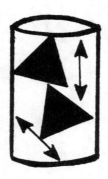

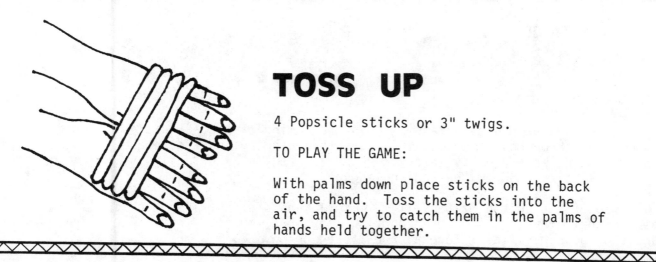

TOSS UP

4 Popsicle sticks or 3" twigs.

TO PLAY THE GAME:

With palms down place sticks on the back of the hand. Toss the sticks into the air, and try to catch them in the palms of hands held together.

STICK GAME

Obtain stirrers from paint stores. Paint one side with designs.

TO PLAY THE GAME:

The stick is tossed into the air. One point is scored for each person or team if the stick lands with the decorated side up.

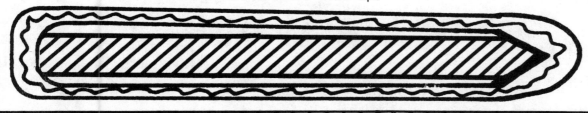

SPEAR IT

Tie a 24" string to a chicken bone or stick. Cut a 1 1/2" diameter hole in a 3" x 3" piece of cardboard. Tie other end of string through the hole in the cardboard.

TO PLAY THE GAME:

Hold the bone and toss cardboard in air. A point is scored each time the bone is speared through the hole in the cardboard.

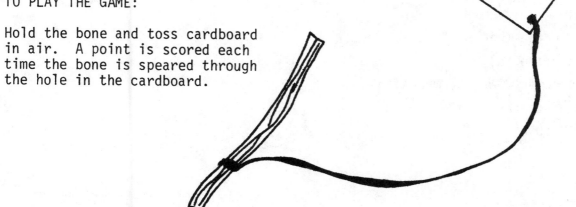

WORD SEARCH

Indian words have been used extensively in the naming of states, cities, rivers, and mountains throughout America. Names, both chosen by the Indian and adapted by the whiteman, were usually descriptive of the region. Our daily use of these names is a lasting bond to the Indian language.

Using a map of the United States, encyclopedias, and dictionaries, find Indian names and their meanings. Make a chart to show what you found out. There are hundreds of possibilities. Several are listed below.

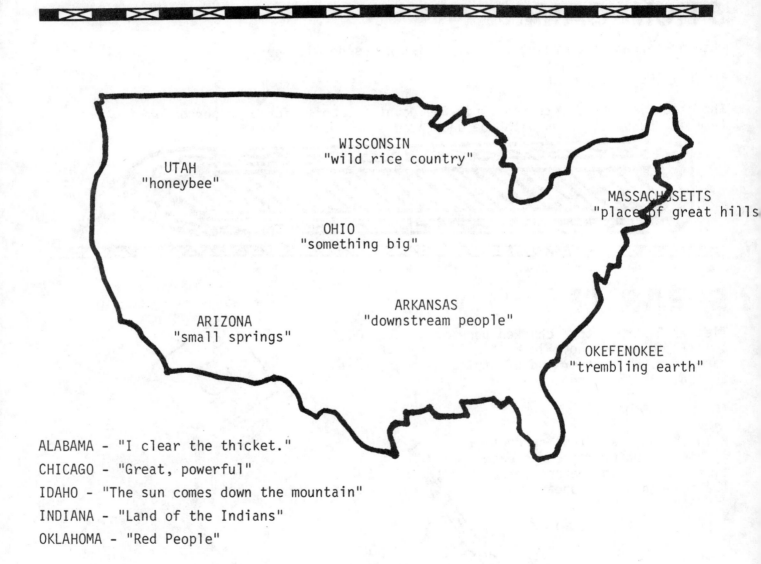

ALABAMA - "I clear the thicket."

CHICAGO - "Great, powerful"

IDAHO - "The sun comes down the mountain"

INDIANA - "Land of the Indians"

OKLAHOMA - "Red People"

Natural Dyes

Colors for clothing, artwork, and body painting were obtained from mineral pigments, clays, bark, roots, twigs, leaves, flowers, weeds, berries and vegetables. For sand painting, these natural sources were pounded into a dry powder. The powder was also combined with buffalo fat for body painting. Clay was used for the same purpose. The main method for extracting color was by boiling in water. Surprisingly, the color obtained is sometimes far different from the original. Try making your own dyes, by boiling for the time shown and then straining.

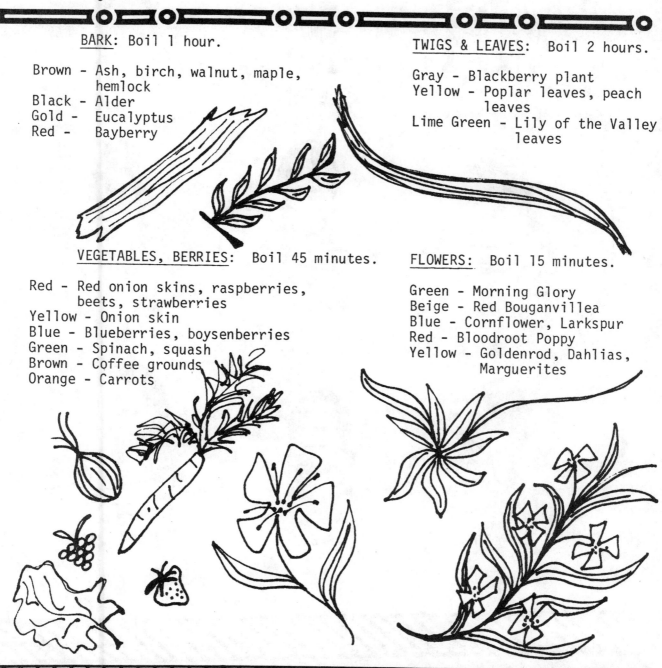

BARK: Boil 1 hour.

Brown - Ash, birch, walnut, maple, hemlock
Black - Alder
Gold - Eucalyptus
Red - Bayberry

TWIGS & LEAVES: Boil 2 hours.

Gray - Blackberry plant
Yellow - Poplar leaves, peach leaves
Lime Green - Lily of the Valley leaves

VEGETABLES, BERRIES: Boil 45 minutes.

Red - Red onion skins, raspberries, beets, strawberries
Yellow - Onion skin
Blue - Blueberries, boysenberries
Green - Spinach, squash
Brown - Coffee grounds
Orange - Carrots

FLOWERS: Boil 15 minutes.

Green - Morning Glory
Beige - Red Bouganvillea
Blue - Cornflower, Larkspur
Red - Bloodroot Poppy
Yellow - Goldenrod, Dahlias, Marguerites

SIGN LANGUAGE

Indians used hand and arm motions to communicate with each other. The Plains tribes used this sign language extensively. The signs were simplistic and designed to be easily understood. Since tribes spoke different languages, sign language became an important communicating tool.

MAN	WOMAN	ME
YOU	WE/ALL	PEOPLE
FRIEND	SEE	GO

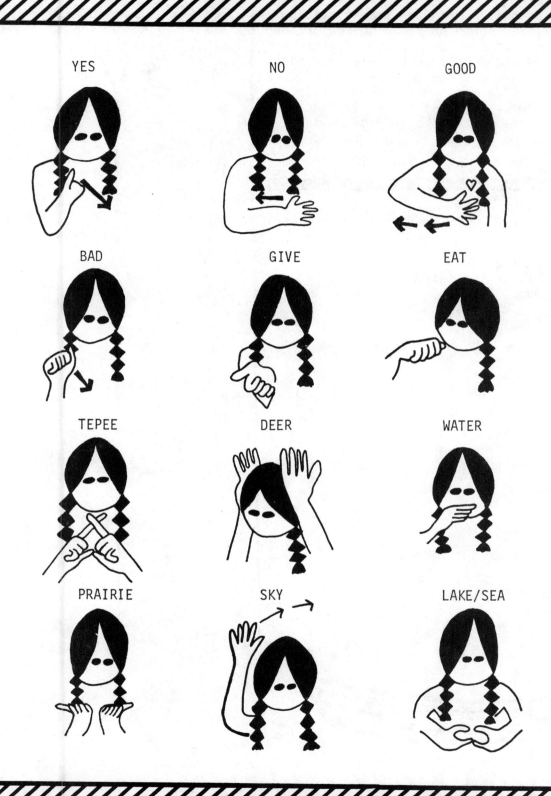

YES   NO   GOOD

BAD   GIVE   EAT

TEPEE   DEER   WATER

PRAIRIE   SKY   LAKE/SEA

CANOE

HISTORICAL AID:

The canoe was used as a means of transportation by Indians all over North America. Canoes ranged in size from ones that held a single person to those that could accommodate 60. They were made in a variety of ways but the two most common were the dugout canoe made from hollowed-out trees and the bullboat made from animal skins stretched around a wooden frame. Canoes were propelled with paddles carved from trees.

MATERIALS:

Cardboard egg carton lid
2 - 10" pieces string or twine
Brown tempera paint
Holepunch   Scissors

DIRECTIONS:

Trace pattern at right onto carton lid.

Cut out and punch holes as shown.

Paint both sides.

Fold on dotted line.

Center string through top hole.

Crisscross and lace through each hole, knotting at bottom. Trim off excess string.

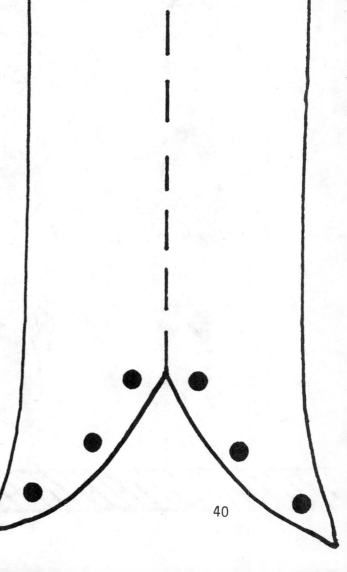

40